LESSER KNOWN MENDIP

Ray Glover

Stimulating walks in the beautiful
South Eastern Mendips

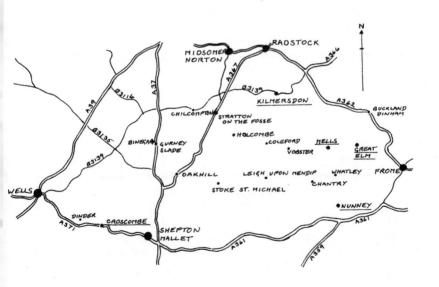

BERKSWELL BOOKS
1995

CONTENTS

ISBN 0 904 631 10 9
© Ray Glover
Published by Berkswell Books
P.O. Box 420, Warminster, Wiltshire
All rights reserved. No part of this publication
may be reproduced without the prior permission
of the publisher

Printed in Great Britain by
Antony Rowe Ltd, Chippenham, Wiltshire

INTRODUCTION

In this book I have assumed that you will be travelling by car, but if you wish to use public transport the following buses serve the area:

BADGERLINE. No. 160 – Wincanton, Bruton, Shepton Mallet, *Croscombe, Dinder,* Wells.

Nos. 161 & 162 – Wells, *Dinder, Croscombe,* Shepton Mallet, *Nunney,* Frome.

No. 184 – Bath, Radstock, Midsomer Norton, *Mells, Great Elm,* Frome.

CLAPTON COACHES. No. 414 *(Monday to Friday only)* – Midsomer Norton, Radstock, *Kilmersdon,* Faulkland, Buckland Dinham, Frome.

Accommodation

If you wish to stay overnight the accommodation offered by the three inns featured in the walks is reputed to be very good. They are: The Talbot in Mells, The George at Nunney, and The Bull Terrier at Croscombe. There are also plenty of other B&B places in the nearby towns and surrounding countryside.

The Maps

I have drawn linear maps to explain the scripts and aligned them, as much as possible, so that you are always walking towards the top of the map.

The maps are only sketch maps and therefore the scales and directions are only approximate. You can follow the routes quite easily using them, but I always find it advisable to carry the appropriate O.S. map for reference. You may spot something of interest off course and wish to go exploring. The walks are covered by the following Ordnance Survey maps: Ordnance Survey, Pathfinder 1:25,000 Series: 1199, 1218 and 1219, or Landranger 1:50,000 Series 183.

The Walks

All the walks are either circular or linear which can be joined together to form various circular ones. For example: Route 1, *or* Routes 1, 2 & 3, *or* Routes 2, 4 & 5.

Apart from two fairly steep climbs in Route 11 the walks are quite easy. In the summer you may have difficulty with stinging nettles growing in the infrequently used footpaths, especially between hedges.

MELLS AND THE SURROUNDING AREA

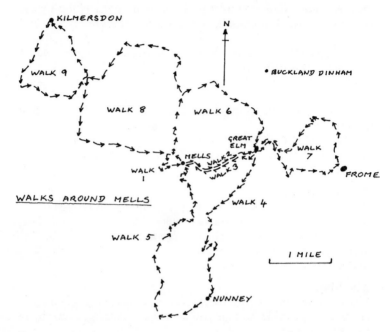

For some reason there are no road signs to let travellers know that they have arrived in Mells. It is an attractive stone built village, set in a meandering wooded valley, on the eastern end of the Mendips.

During the sixteenth century it was acquired by the Horner family (reputedly of 'Little Jack Horner' fame). There are many unsubstantiated versions of the story behind the nursery rhyme. According to one of them the Abbot of Glastonbury sent to King Henry VIII the deeds of Mells Manor, hidden in a pie, as a bribe to prevent the dissolution of Glastonbury Abbey. But the messenger, Jack Horner, removed them (the plum) and kept them for himself. His descendants still own much of the village.

In the early part of the eighteenth century the village owed much of its prosperity to the woollen industry which was centred three miles to the east around Frome. In 1744 John Horner leased land downstream of the village to James Fussell who established the Iron Works between Mells and Great Elm. Edged tools were forged there until 1895. You will pass these overgrown ruins on the very attractive walk along the Mells Stream.

COUNTRYSIDE NEAR FROME

The Fussells also set up factories at Great Elm, Chantry, Railford and Nunney, which is another very beautiful village, with its ruined castle, seventeenth-century pub and old cottages with unusual names.

To the north west of Mells is Kilmersdon which is reputed to be the home of 'Jack and Jill', who fetched 'the pail of water'.

The area was also part of the Somerset Coal-field, with mines at Mells, Vobster, Newbury, Buckland Dinham and other neighbouring villages. To transport the coal from this valley a branch line to the aborted Dorset and Somerset Canal was started but never finished. Its remains can be seen to the north of Mells at Conduit Bridge, to the east in Vallis Vale and to the west at Upper Vobster. On nearby Barrow Hill clumps of trees grow on the site of the 'Machine' or 'Lever' Lock patented by James Fussell.

Eventually a railway was built from Frome to Radstock, with a branch line from Mells station (near Mells coal mine) to Vobster and Newbury. These lines have since closed and the branch has almost disappeared, but enthusiasts are at present trying to have the line from Frome to Radstock preserved.

ROUTE 1. Around Mells Village (O.S. 730490). (With modifications for wheelchairs.) (1.5 miles.)

Most of the village is in a conservation area and contains many beautiful buildings of architectural and historical interest. In the spring every garden, bank and grassy verge seems to be crammed with daffodils. The Daffodil Fair, which is held every Easter Monday, is well worth a visit.

(1) Parking is difficult in Mells. I find the most convenient place is around the junction of five roads on the eastern end of the village by the village post office.

The 'bus shelter' at this junction is in fact a *Community Water Tap and Shelter* designed by Sir Edwin Lutyens (the architect of New Delhi and designer of the Cenotaph in Whitehall) as a memorial to Mark Horner. When Mark died in 1908 his mother, Lady Horner, had water from the Manor reservoir laid on to various points in the village.

(2) As you walk up the hill towards the main street the large building on your left was a seventeenth-century *Clothier's Mansion*.

(3) At the next junction is the *War Memorial* designed by Lutyens. It is the most democratic memorial I've ever seen. Everybody is in alphabetical order, with no mention of rank or social standing.

(4) Keep to the main road. The building in the yard on your left is the fifteenth century *Tythe Barn*.

(5) Just before the inn turn right into *New Street*. New Street was built in the fifteenth century. Apparently there are records of the Abbot of Glastonbury, John Selwood, compensating the Rector of Mells for encroaching on his land when building 'Nywe-billyng' (New Street). The boys' school on the right was built in 1840.

(6) At the end of New Street is *Saint Andrew's Church*. This fifteenth century church, a fine example of Somerset perpendicular style, is built of oolitic limestone. On one of my visits I was lucky enough to be given a conducted tour of the tower by Mr. Potter, the clock winder. As well as housing a peal of eight bells it contains an old faceless clock which strikes the hours and the quarters. Every three hours, starting at midnight, it plays one of four tunes. One of the four, 'The Mells Tune', is of ancient but unknown date. The earliest mention of this clock is 1658. To appreciate the full beauty of this church it is best to buy a guide sheet from just inside the door. Among the notable features are the large tapestry by Lady Horner to a design by Sir Edward Burne-Jones; the memorial to Raymond Asquith, son of the Liberal Prime Minister, who married Katherine Horner (she inherited the Horner estates from her brother, Edward); the

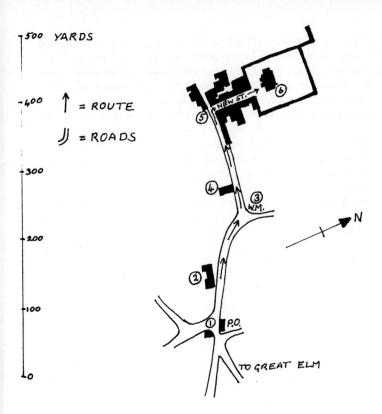

carved tablet, designed by Burne-Jones, depicting a peacock, in memory of Laura Lyttleton who was sister of Margot Asquith and wife of Alfred Lyttleton, Cabinet Minister and England cricketer; the horse and rider memorial to Edward Horner who was killed in the First World War (the statue in the first sculptural work carried out by Sir Alfred Munnings, the equestrian painter; the plinth of the statue was designed by Sir Edwin Lutyens); the carved stone panels above the altar; in the grave-yard, the stones of Sir John and Lady Horner were designed by Lutyens.

Nearby there are the graves of Ronald Knox and Siegfried Sassoon. Knox was the Roman Catholic priest and scholar who worked on his translation of The Bible while living in Mells. He died in 1957. Siegfried Sassoon, who wished to be buried hear Knox, was the First World War poet and author. He died in 1967. Lady Violet Bonham Carter, who died in 1969, is also buried in the churchyard.

Lutyens also designed the McKenna family tomb. Reginald McKenna, the banker and Liberal MP, was born in 1863. In 1908, the year he married Pamela Jekyll, he was appointed First Lord of the Admiralty. He later became Chancellor of the Exchequer. His wife was a very accomplished musician and, during his terms of office, one of the most popular hostesses in political circles. He died in September 1943. A few months later his widow was killed when she fell out of a moving train at Wimbledon.

On the south side of the church there are two very old yews, and on the north side an avenue of yews leads, through an ingenious stile, to the open fields beyond.

(7) After leaving the church retrace your steps down New Street and turn right to the *Talbot*. This fifteenth-century coaching inn is well worth a visit for its ancient buildings and courtyard, its real ales and home cooked meals. I often have a meal, ask the landlord's permission to park, and start my walks from there.

(8) Next to the inn car park on the right is *The Manor House* and grounds. The present Elizabethan house stands on the site of a grange of the Abbot of Glastonbury who owned it in the mid sixteenth century before the Horners acquired it on the dissolution of Glastonbury Abbey. The original Elizabethan building was an H planned house and over twice the size of the building we see today. The north wing and central section were demolished in the eighteenth century. About that time the Horners moved out. The house was used as a farm house for a time and then as a trade school. In the nineteenth century the Horners returned, and since then the house has been extensively restored with the help of Sir Edwin Lutyens. He also co-operated with Gertrude Jekyll (any relation to Reginald McKenna's wife?) with the design of the gardens. The manor is now the home of the Earl and Countess of Oxford and Asquith.

(9) Turn left opposite the Manor gates where two heraldic dogs stand guard. As you do so, on the left you can catch a glimpse of
(10) the eighteenth century former *Rectory* and its attractive grounds. Time seems to have stood still as you walk up this street with its thatched cottages and stone pavement. Look out on the left for
(11) the old *Drinking Fountain* built of strangely weathered 'worm-eaten' stone. On the opposite side of the road is the eighteenth
(12) century *Lock Up*. The last detainee was Teddy Allwood who was described as the parish jester and drunk.

Main Route

Turn right at the lock up, go to the end of the lane and then take the sunken footpath down the hill. The derelict building on the

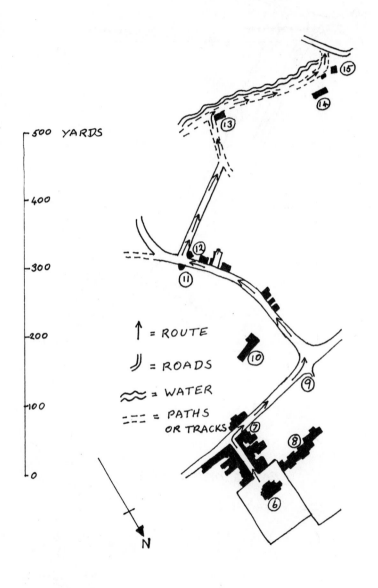

500 YARDS

400

300

200

100

0

↑ = ROUTE
)) = ROADS
≈ = WATER
--- = PATHS OR TRACKS

N

9

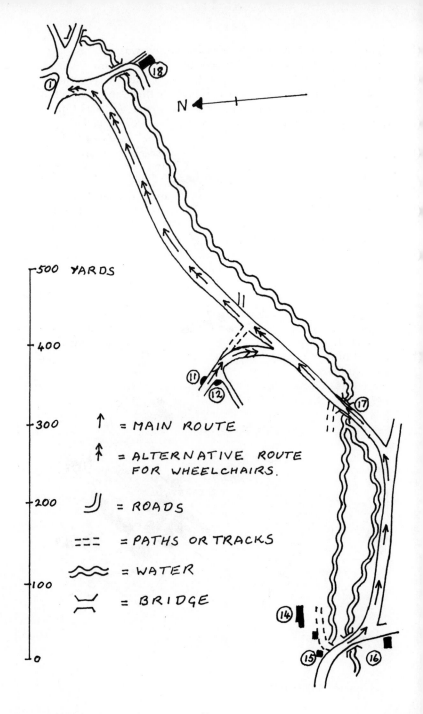

N

500 YARDS

400

↑ = MAIN ROUTE

⬆ = ALTERNATIVE ROUTE
FOR WHEELCHAIRS.

300

⌇ = ROADS

200

═══ = PATHS OR TRACKS

〰〰 = WATER

100

⤳⤳ = BRIDGE

0

10

13) right at the bottom was the *Bell Inn* which was also used as a
court room. Turn right and follow the path upstream. Near the
14) end set back under the rock face is a large old house, which is
called *Bilboa Cottage* on the parish map. Is there any connection
with the old Bilboa coal mine which was near Vobster? On the
15) right as you join the road are the remains of *Mells Flour Mill*.

When you join the road go over the bridge. As you do so you
16) can see *Mells Park* on your right. Lutyens designed Mells Park
House for Reginald McKenna after the old house was destroyed
by fire in 1917.

Follow the road around to the left and then take the next
17) turning left. Go past the regimented poplars, over a small bridge,
and then turn right. At the end of the road turn left to the starting
point. If you make a small detour by turning right instead of left
18) you will see the eighteenth century *Almshouses* on the next bend.

Alternative Route For Wheelchairs
Go down the hill, keeping to the road (the path is too steep) and
then turn sharp left just before you reach the bottom. At the end
of this quiet valley road turn left and you should find yourself
back at the start. If you make a small detour by turning right
18) instead of left you will see the eighteenth-century *Almshouses* on
the next bend.

Mells is such an attractive and interesting village I am sure that
any modifications you make to this route will be beneficial.

Continue with Route 2 or 6.

MELLS LOCKUP.

ROUTE 2. River Walk from Mells (O.S. 730490) **to Great Elm** (O.S. 748491) **via Fussell's Iron Works**. 'Black Satanic Mills Turned Green'. (2.2 miles.) (The first mile is suitable for wheelchairs.)

(1)   Start your walk from the five way road junction by Mells Post Office and take the road sign-posted Great Elm and Frome. The wall on the right as you leave the village is capped with old grind stones from Fussell's Iron Works.

(2)   When the road bends to the left turn down the track to the right. This will take you through the wooded gorge, cut by the Mells Stream, where Fussell started his tool-making empire. In the spring the valley is a mass of snowdrops and in early summer there are monkshoods and dames violets. Also in early spring we heard a blackcap and saw holly blue butterflies which had been fooled by the warm weather. About half a mile down the track you will start seeing evidence of the industrial past. Were the small buildings on the left workers' houses or small workshops?

(3)   Soon after this there are some large buildings in front of you. At this point those in wheelchairs will have to turn round and go back unless their chairs are robust and their pushers strong. The footpath goes to the left of the buildings and then carries on between a rockface and a high wall. Between this wall and the river bank lies the main part of *Fussell's Iron Works*.

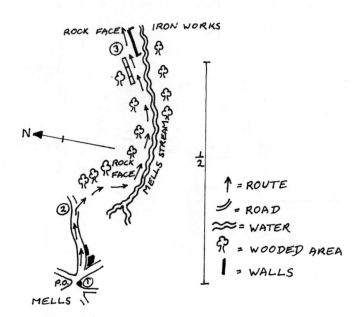

Plan of Iron Works

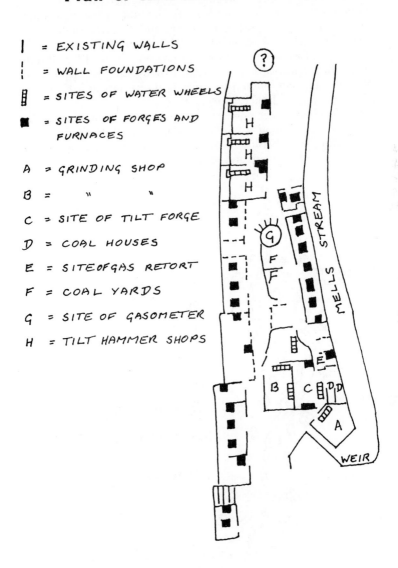

| = EXISTING WALLS
¦ = WALL FOUNDATIONS
▯ = SITES OF WATER WHEELS
■ = SITES OF FORGES AND FURNACES

A = GRINDING SHOP
B =   "   "
C = SITE OF TILT FORGE
D = COAL HOUSES
E = SITE OF GAS RETORT
F = COAL YARDS
G = SITE OF GASOMETER
H = TILT HAMMER SHOPS

Water power was used to drive the trip hammers, bellows and other machines. The report I read in Frome Library of excavations carried out by *BIAS* in 1975 explains most of the structures but what was the circular pit next to the trip hammers?

James Fussell started forging edge tools here when he was granted a 99-year lease in 1744. By the end of the eighteenth century they were exporting to Europe and America. In the early 1800s the works had extended enough to need nine water wheels to drive the forges, hammers and grindstones. In an 1803 edition of the *Bristol Journal* it is recorded that during the Napoleonic Wars the Fussells offered to give the Government 1000 pikes initially and then 2000 each week thereafter.

In the 1860s water power was replaced by steam to drive the machinery, including a new rolling mill. In 1894 the business was sold to Isaac Nash of Worcestershire who closed the factory and auctioned the plant and machinery.

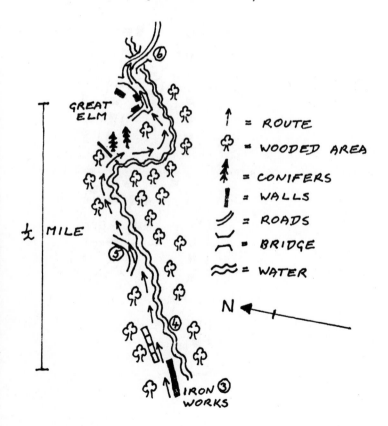

Mells Stream at Great Elm

As you continue along the footpath after passing between the high wall and the rock face you will see more evidence of small industrial buildings on your left. Many of the retaining walls are built of clinker.

(4) Near the end of this terrace there is a wooden rail on the right. If you look over this you can see the outlet of the system of water ducts supplying power to the works.

(5) When you reach the service road to the houses on the hillside follow the Wyvern Way footpath towards Frome. The path follows the stream for about half a mile where it goes up the hill to join one of the back streets of Great Elm. Go down the road, past Glenthorne to cross the bridge over Mells Stream.

(6)

Continue with Routes 3, 4 or 7.

ROUTE 3. The Bridge at Great Elm (O.S. 748491) to **Mells** (O.S. 730490) (2.2 miles.)

To get to the bridge turn off the Mells to Frome road in the village of Great Elm. Take the narrow steep road which is opposite the green. Park your car near the bridge on the opposite side of the river from the village of Great Elm. Climb over the

(1) stile at the end of the upstream parapet of the bridge.

Take the track which leads to the railway. Just before the railway track cross over the footbridge on the right, turn right, and then follow the path up the valley keeping Mells Stream in sight to your right.

(2) There is an interesting rock face along this path showing tilted strata caused by prehistoric upheavals. In these upheavals the strata were raised and folded to form a dome. Streams eroded the north slope of this dome to form the valleys through Mells, Whatley Bottom and Murder Combe. The present streams are probably relics of much more powerful watercourses of the late glacial age. This may account for the depth and steepness of these valleys.

(3) After just over half a mile cross over the stream by the footbridge and turn left. Keep to the left of 'Treetops' gateway. Continue upstream.

(4) The wooden guardrail marks the outlet of the water ducting system which supplied power to *Fussell's Iron Works*. After passing remains of small industrial buildings on your right go between the high wall and the rock face. On the other side of this wall is

(5) the *Fussell's Iron Works (see Route 2 for details)*.

Continue on upstream, past more small industrial ruins on your right, until the track meets the road.

(6) Turn left and follow the road into Mells. The wall on the left as you enter the village is capped with old grindstones from the ironworks.

Continue with Routes 1, 2 or 6.

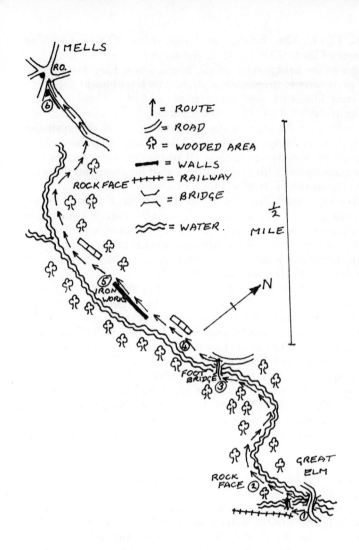

MELLS
P.O.

↑ = ROUTE
╱╱ = ROAD
♧ = WOODED AREA
▬ = WALLS
+++ = RAILWAY
⤝ = BRIDGE
≋ = WATER.

ROCK FACE

½ MILE

N

⑤
IRON WORKS

FOOT BRIDGE
③

④

GREAT ELM

ROCK FACE ②

①

17

ROUTE 4. The Bridge at Great Elm (O.S. 748491) **to Nunney Castle** (O.S. 737457). (4.3 miles.)

To get to the bridge turn off the Mells, Great Elm, Frome road and go down the steep, narrow street which is opposite the green in Great Elm. Park your car near the end of the bridge on the opposite side of the river from the village.

(1) Climb over the stile by the gate at the end of the upstream parapet of the bridge and take the small, fairly steep footpath up through the woods on your left. (If you see the railway track you have gone too far.) Turn right at the top of the slope and this path
(2) will take you to the road at Murder Combe.

Murder Combe has been so called since Saxon times. According to John Strachey, the eighteenth century historian, it got its name when prisoners were killed after a battle for Tedbury Camp on top of the hill. As Strachey tended to get carried away by his imagination, the name is more likely to be a derivative of Mordrancombe after an ancient chieftain.

Turn left and then, after a few yards, cross the road and go over the stile by the barbed wire 'gate' on the right. Go along the remains of a lane, and follow the hedge and fence towards Whatley church on the horizon. In the corner of the field climb over the stile to the left of the ash tree. Stay on the left-hand side of the hedge and keep going towards the church, past the drinking trough, and on to the far corner of the next field.

Get over the stile on the right and turn left. Go through the gap into the next field and bear left to the stile which is to the left
(3) of the wall under the yew tree. Take the narrow path between the bungalow and house, through a flimsy gate, into the drive. After a short distance go through the gap in the wall on the left and go down the footpath, past the house on the left, to the lane. When you reach the lane go on to the main road and turn left and then
(4) right towards the Sun Inn.

Go past the Sun Inn and the Moon Out into the field. Pass as close as possible to the water trough in the middle of the field as you make for the dead looking tree showing above the near
(5) horizon. Get into the next field through a broken kissing gate which is in the corner slightly to your right as you go down the slope.

(6) Go past the tree and leave the field via the gate which is to the left of the far corner. Turn left away from the main road. When the road bends into a hollow turn down the track to the right.

(7) In 1837 a Roman villa was discovered at the end of Whiteway Lane, downstream of the bridge. The landowner erected a curiously shaped shed to protect a mosaic pavement. Fortunately he also commissioned a coloured drawing before it was

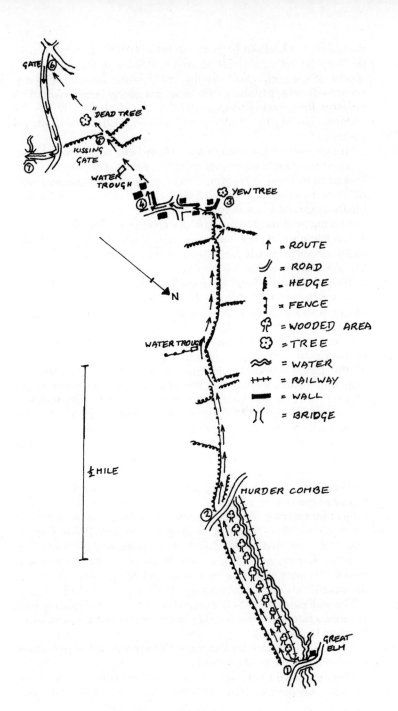

GATE ⑥

"DEAD TREE"

KISSING GATE ⑤

⑦

WATER TROUGH

④

③ YEW TREE

N

↑ = ROUTE

= ROAD

= HEDGE

= FENCE

= WOODED AREA

= TREE

= WATER

= RAILWAY

= WALL

)(= BRIDGE

WATER TROUGH

½ MILE

MURDER COMBE

②

GREAT ELM

①

completely vandalised by souvenir hunters. The drawing is now in Taunton Archaeological Museum at Taunton Castle. A stone model of the bath suite was also made at the same time and is now in Frome Museum. The site has since been returfed to preserve the remaining specimens.

After crossing the bridge turn right and follow the footpath upstream.

At this point I saw some Giant Hogweeds which were about three metres high (they can grow to four). The flower heads looked to be about 30 centimetres in diameter. If you can see any of these be careful, as contact with them can cause severe skin blisters, especially in sunlight.

The footpath takes you past the sewage works into an open area with horse jumps and then into a rough meadow as the valley closes in. In the early summer this meadow was a mass of Ox Eye Daisies and Red Campion.

(8) Turn up the drive away from the farm and then follow the high wall which surrounds *Nunney Court*. We were very lucky on one of our walks to see a peacock putting on a magnificent display from its perch on this wall.

In the grounds of Nunney Court the remains of Fussell's iron works lie 'rusting away'. John Fussell, son of James Fussell III of Mells, started making spades, shovels and edge tools at Nunney sometime prior to 1791. The Fussells continued to manufacture tools ('The best in the county, perhaps in the kingdom') in Nunney until about 1895. Many garden walls in the locality are capped with worn out Fussell's grindstones cut in half.

When you reach the main street (Frome Road) turn right. Go past the stream on the right and the church on the left.

(9) The *Nunney Cross* was removed to Whatley many years ago until it was recovered, restored and re-erected in its present riverside site between the castle and church. Money was raised for this project by reviving the old Nunney Fair which is now an annual

(10) event on the first Saturday in August. *Nunney Parish Church*, which is dedicated to All Saints, is of unknown antiquity but there is a fragment of a Saxon cross in the chancel and a Norman font at the west end. The nave, transepts and chancel are of the thirteenth and fourteenth centuries. The tower is fifteenth century.

The wall painting of St. George is one of the few depicting him without a horse (there is another in the chapel in Farleigh Castle, Farleigh Hungerford).

The fourteenth century knight in the window sill is probably a member of the de la Mare family.

The knight and lady on a table tomb are probably Sir John Poulet, who died in 1436, and his wife Constance. The tomb

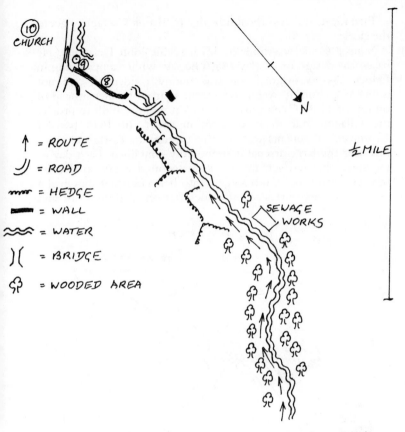

originally stood free from the wall in the body of the church. It was moved at some date a little later than 1791 to its present cramped position. To fit it between another monument and the wall one end was removed. One side now touches the north wall and so is hidden from view.

The gentleman and lady of the Elizabethan period on a tomb chest are probably Richard Prater, who bought the castle in 1577, and his wife.

The screen across the chancel arch was once across the south transept arch. It was removed to Bath until it was rediscovered in 1876 and put into its present position by the Somerset Archaeological Society. To fit it into place they could not avoid building it off-centre. To disguise this the centre aisle was repositioned. The pattern of its tracery heads has been dated to the beginning of the fifteenth century.

Just outside the west door is the Fussell tomb.

Turn right and cross the footbridge by Brook Cottage to get to the castle.

(11)   *Nunney Castle* was built in 1373 by Sir John Delamere. He based the design on castles which he saw while campaigning in France. As its original use was purely residential, and not military, he built it over a convenient source of water instead of on top of a hill. Cynics maintain that it was not built to protect the villagers but to keep them in order. In 1645 two of Cromwell's regiments were sent to capture the castle and commandeer the large arsenal it supposedly contained. Each day of the siege the garrison in the castle tortured a pig so that its squeals would fool the besiegers into believing that they had a plentiful supply of fresh meat. A deserter revealed their ruse and

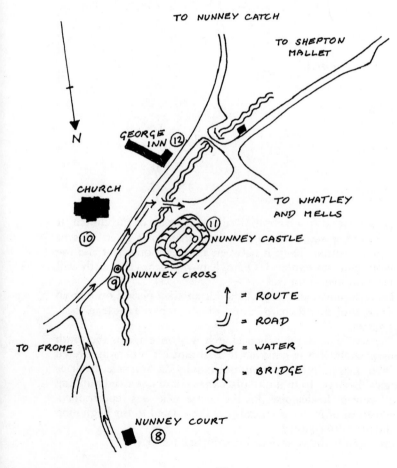

pointed out the section of wall which was weakened by a built-in stairway. The Roundheads soon breached the defences when they bombarded this spot. A cannon ball can be seen on display in the church.

The centre of Nunney is a conservation area and contains many picturesque cottages, mainly eighteenth century. In the early 1960s, before heavy vehicles were re-routed away from the village, it was possible to buy these buildings for as little as £50 each. It's a different story now. In 1950 the castle, together with the title 'Lord of the Manor' was sold by auction for £600.

(12)   The *George Inn*, which is a seventeenth century building on a fourteenth-century site, was closed by the brewery in 1968 but luckily it was bought, extended and re-opened as a free house. This is another inn worth visiting for its pleasant atmosphere, friendly service, real ale and good home-cooked meals. The bar meals are excellent but it is worth visiting the restaurant just to see its magnificent ceiling. It is in the form of a series of canopies made of wooden panels. In the corners of each canopy there are the crests associated with the castle. The inn sign which spans the street is the only one of its kind left in the county.

Continue with Route 5 from the castle.

ROUTE 5. Nunney Castle (O.S. 737457) **to Mells Post Office** (O.S. 730490) **via Chantry Pond and Railford Iron Works**. (6 miles.)

Park your car in the short street which leads to the castle, or, if you intend having a pub lunch, ask if you can use The George's car park.

(1)   After looking around the castle, (see Route 4), go up the short street in front of you. Cross over the road at the end and go up Horn Street which is diagonally in front of you.

(2)   At the bottom of Horn Street is the *Nineteenth Century Lock Up*.

(3)   Further up, some of the cottages were once *Weavers' Dwellings*. Some still have square holes in the ceilings to accommodate the lengths of cloth as they were manufactured. Tennis rackets were

(4)   also made in Horn Street. As you continue up the hill the *Old Mill* on the left is where flour was once ground and, in more

(5)   recent times, cider was pressed. Near the top of the hill is *Rockfield House*. It was built in 1804 and gets its name from the adjoining Rack Field where cloth was stretched and dried.

    Leave the village, go past the road from the left and, when

(6)   you reach a T-junction turn right. Cross over to the left-hand side of the road and when the road bends sharply to the right take the track with high hedges in front of you.

NUNNEY LOCKUP

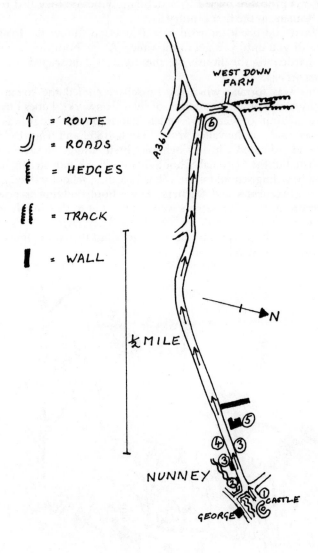

WEST DOWN FARM

↑ = ROUTE

⌒ = ROADS

≀ = HEDGES

≀≀ = TRACK

▮ = WALL

A 361

⑥

½ MILE

⊢→N

⑤

④ ③

③

NUNNEY

② ① CASTLE

GEORGE

In 1869 an urn was discovered under an old yew tree on *West Down Farm*, the entrance to which you have just passed on the left. It contained a hoard of 10 gold, 232 silver and 4 brass coins and was probably buried by a rich family before they fled from the Romans in the first century.

(7) When you reach the road at a T-junction follow the road in front of you until you get to the valley. At the bottom of the hill the garden to the house on the right is landscaped around

(8) *Chantry Pond*.

This was formed when the Fussells dammed the stream to supply water power to another of their ironworks. James Fussell VI was vicar of Chantry, which stands on the ridge on the opposite side of the valley, from 1846 to 1852 and from 1877 to 1879. He founded Chantry School which, under the same roof, consisted of the National School, infant school, industrial school and a boarding school for girls. The boarding school trained girls to be governesses and teachers. The school building is now a furniture store. When repairs were carried out to the church deep pits were found under the chancel floor. They were to be used as a family vault for generations of Fussells but the family line died out before it could be used.

RAILFORD IRONWORKS

When the road turns sharp left go through the gate in front of you and follow the track along the valley floor. The swampy area which you pass on your left was Railford Pond until the dam gave way a few years ago. This was yet another power supply to another ironworks. I think the ruins in the garden of the house on the opposite bank as you approach the road must be the Railford Works.

(9)

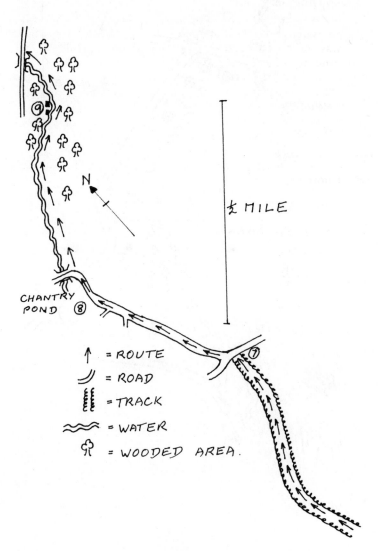

½ MILE

CHANTRY POND ⑧

↑ = ROUTE

⫽ = ROAD

⫿ = TRACK

〰 = WATER

♧ = WOODED AREA.

N

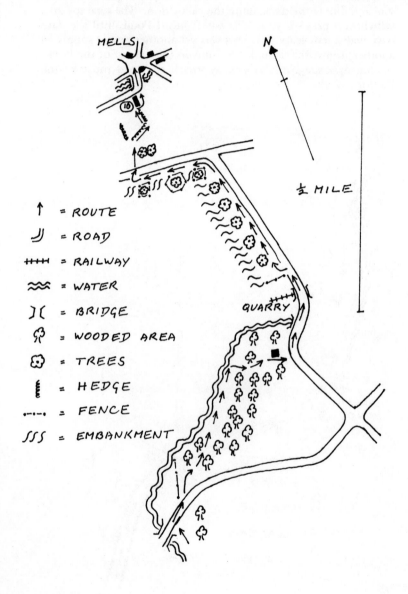

MELLS

N

½ MILE

↑ = ROUTE

⌡ = ROAD

+++ = RAILWAY

≈ = WATER

)(= BRIDGE

🌳 = WOODED AREA

❀ = TREES

❳ = HEDGE

-·-·- = FENCE

ʃʃʃ = EMBANKMENT

QUARRY

When you reach the road turn right and walk up the hill for about 70 yards. Just before the road bends to the right turn left and follow the track into the wood. At the bottom of the slope follow the footpath along the bank of the stream until you reach the quarry buildings.

Turn right and climb the steps cut into the hillside. Near the top there are some large yew trees. Their size indicate that they are over 1,000 years old. They were coppiced many years ago, probably to provide bows for a nearby garrison. At the top bear left, go past a large metal water tank, and then down a slope into the road.

Turn left, down hill, past the quarry exit, over the railway bridge, up the hill and past the quarry entrance.

Climb over the stile on the left and follow the footpath which runs parallel to the road. Get over the stile or through the gate into the field at the end.

Follow the right-hand hedge around to the left. After passing three fenced plantations on your left and a gate on your right look for a clump of shrubs growing out from the hedge. Climb over the stile just beyond the shrubs.

Bear right as you cross the road and get over the stile into the field. Make for the hedge below the clump of trees slightly to your right. Keep the hedge on your left as you follow the footpath arrow to the right.

10) At the next corner, climb over the stile, go downhill, over the stile in the bottom corner and follow the path in front of the eighteenth-century *Almshouses* mentioned in Route 1.

As you go over the old stone bridge the five-way road junction and Mells Post Office are in front of you.

Continue with Routes 1, 2, or 6.

ROUTE 6. Mells to Great Elm Bridge via Conduit Bridge and Barrow Hill. (4 miles.)

(1)   Start your walk from the five-way road junction by the Post Office. Walk up the main road, past the *Clothiers' Mansion*, to the *War Memorial* as in Route 1. Turn right at the memorial and then climb over the stile into the field on the left.

Make for the right hand corner of the churchyard wall. Go along the wall to the gate in front of you. On the way have a look (2) at the ingenious stile from the churchyard.

Turn right through the gate, go up the hill and skirt around the left hand side of the young trees at the top. Follow the hedge around to the left until you reach the stile under the beech tree. Climb over into the corner of the next field and go straight ahead to the stone stile in the hedge facing you. Climb over and go straight up the road.

I found large bunches of the Common Star of Bethlehem along these verges.

(3)   As you go over the railway bridge (Conduit Bridge) you will see a long depression just uphill of, and parallel to the track. This is the remains of the branch line of the *Dorset & Somerset Canal*. I think the clump of trees and bushes in the field on the right is growing on the site of one of the locks.

The footpath which is supposed to lead to Hill House Farm from half way up the hill has disappeared. As there is no real advantage in using it, I should follow the road up the hill and (4) then take the right hand fork. Take the first track to the right. (5) This will take you to Hill House Farm. Skirt around to the right of the farm buildings and then keep to the left hand fence until you reach the gate into the lane. Go down the lane.

The field on the left is marked 'Bull Pit Ground' on the O.S. map. It could be either the site of ancient bull baiting contests or an unproductive coal mine. ('Bull' is old English slang for dud or useless e.g. army bull). The chimney you can see in the valley is part of the buildings around a disused mine shaft.

At the end of the lane climb over the stile into the path with high hedges. At the end of the path get over the log fence into the field and go straight on. Follow the left hand fence until you reach the stile. The village across the valley on the left is Buckland Dinham. Go over the stile and then bear slightly right to the next stile. Climb over this stile and bear right again so that you are going straight downhill.

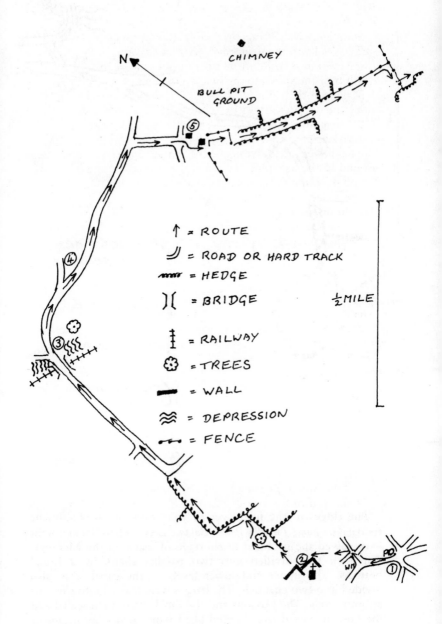

CHIMNEY

BULL PIT GROUND

N

↑ = ROUTE

⌡ = ROAD OR HARD TRACK

﹀﹀﹀ = HEDGE

)(= BRIDGE

‡ = RAILWAY

❀ = TREES

▬ = WALL

≈ = DEPRESSION

•••• = FENCE

½ MILE

31

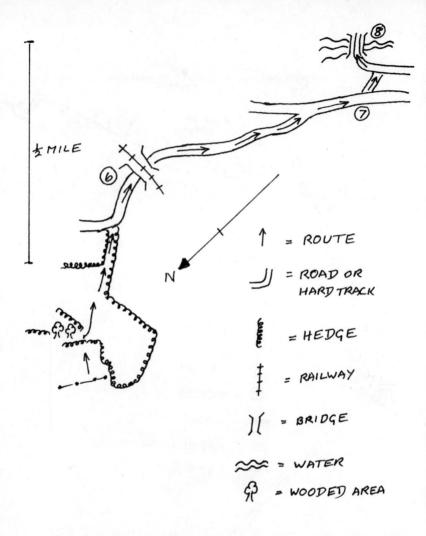

½ MILE

↑ = ROUTE

⌐⌐ = ROAD OR HARD TRACK

§ = HEDGE

‡ = RAILWAY

)(= BRIDGE

≈≈ = WATER

♧ = WOODED AREA

The ridges in the field over to your right are probably the remains of *James Fussell's Patent Balance Locks*. These locks might have solved the problem of shortage of water in the Mendips. The lock was divided into two parallel shafts by a broad buttress. The upper and lower levels of the canal were also divided into two channels. The barges were floated into caissons at both levels. The caissons and the canals were then sealed and the caissons raised and lowered like balance scales, by means of an arrangement of chains and pulleys attached to a beam across the buttress. The speed of descent of the caissons could be regulated by the amount of water added to the caisson at the upper level. Unfortunately the canal was never finished, so the locks were never fully tested, but a similar device was later used on the Grand Western Canal between Taunton and Burlescombe.

In the corner of the field get over the stile by the gate into the lane. Follow the lane to the road. Carry straight on, under the bridge which seems to be built for wide vehicles with narrow wheel bases, into the village of Great Elm.

Turn right when you reach the main road. After a while turn left and go down the steep path which has an iron barrier at the top. When you reach the road turn sharp left and go down to the bridge.

Follow Routes 3, 4, or 7.

BRIDGE BELOW
BARROW HILL

ROUTE 7. Circular Walk from Great Elm Bridge via outskirts of Frome, Spring Gardens, Vallis Vale and Bedlam. (5.2 miles.)

To get to the bridge turn off the Mells to Frome road in the village of Great Elm. Take the narrow steep road which is opposite the green.

(1)   Start your walk from the end of the bridge opposite the village of Great Elm. Follow the road up the hill to the sharp right hand bend. Go through the gate in front of you and make for the stile into the woods straight ahead.

Go through the woods until the footpath meets the bed of the old railway track. Turn right onto it and follow it under a bridge and over the bridge which crosses the Mells Stream. Bear right
(2)   and follow the waterside path past two old lime kilns on your left.

Lime was made from limestone which was mixed with coke and dropped into the top of the kilns. The heat from the burning coke decomposed the limestone (calcium carbonate) to produce quicklime (calcium oxide) and carbon dioxide. Tramps were sometimes asphyxiated by the carbon dioxide when they sheltered in warm kilns at night. The lime produced was very impure and was slaked by adding water to form calcium hydroxide, and used in whitewash, mortar, cement and as a soil conditioner.

(3)   When you reach the old quarry go past the first bridge which is blocked by a large boulder.

Follow the footpath over the next bridge on the right but before you do so, see how excavations have revealed strata of two distinctly different rocks in the rock face on your left on the opposite side of the quarry. (You will be able to have a closer look later on, near the end of the walk.)

Follow the tributary upstream through the wooded valley past another disused quarry. Climb over the stile and then at the end of the path turn sharp left up the hill.

(4)   Just before the house climb over the stile by the gate on the right. Go straight ahead, keeping the fence to your right. Get over the next stile and carry straight on past the high security fence around the lorry park.

Climb over the stile in the corner of the field. Cross over the road and turn right. Just before the post box turn left down Whatcombe Road.

When you reach the end of the houses on the left-hand side of the road, climb over the stile on the left, opposite Upper Whatcombe. Go straight down the hill to the stile in the corner
(5)   of the field. Climb over and turn left.

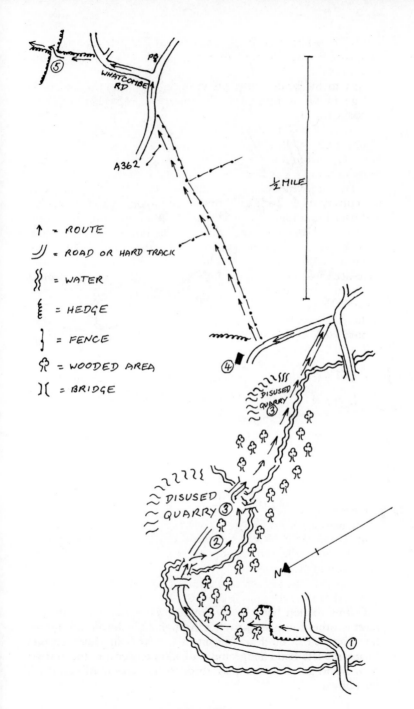

= ROUTE

= ROAD OR HARD TRACK

= WATER

= HEDGE

= FENCE

= WOODED AREA

= BRIDGE

WHATCOMBE RD

A362

PO

½ MILE

DISUSED QUARRY

DISUSED QUARRY

N

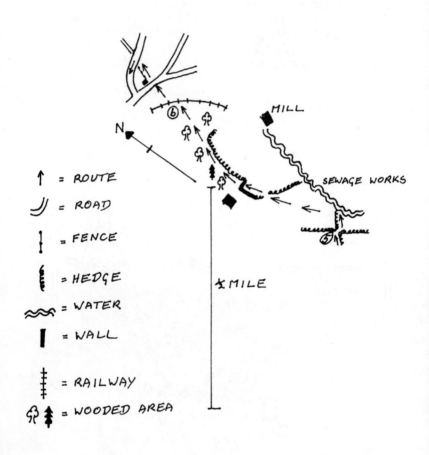

Follow the left hand hedge down towards the river until you
meet another footpath; turn left through a pinch stile and follow
this footpath through a gate into the next field. Turn left and
follow the left-hand hedge and wall. Climb over the stile in front
of you and go along the path through the trees until you reach
(6) the railway.

Cross the track, bearing slightly left, and get over the stile into the field. Go straight down across the field and into the road. Cross the road, climb over the stile into the field in front of you. Get over the stile on the opposite side of the field into the road and turn left.

(7) Turn right by the first house on the right and then follow the raised track across the field. Turn left just before the barn and skirt the edge of the field, keeping the barn and Old Mill to your right. Go past the sluice gate and then go over the footbridge on the right into the next field. Bear left and make for the footbridge by the farmhouse. Cross over the bridge and turn left.

Follow the track to the main road and turn left. Climb up the hill over the river bridge and the railway bridge and turn right, over the stile by the parapet. At the end of the fenced footpath alongside the railway track turn left over the stile, and continue on upstream. Keep to the left of the small arch by the weir.

(8) The structure you are now on is the remains of the *Murtry Aqueduct* which carried the branch line of the Dorset and Somerset Canal. The canal was planned to run from the Kennet & Avon Canal at Widbrook, through Frome and Wincanton, to

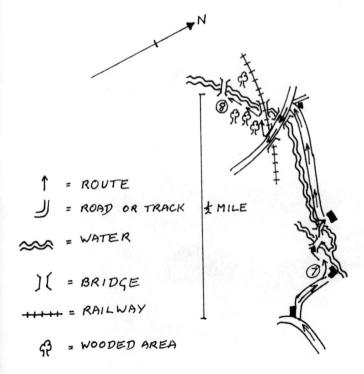

↑ = ROUTE

⌡⌡ = ROAD OR TRACK   ⊢ MILE

∼∼∼ = WATER

)(= BRIDGE

+++++ = RAILWAY

🌳 = WOODED AREA

the Dorset Stour near Sturminster Newton, with the branch line from Nettlebridge to Frome. Unfortunately it was never completed. (*See Route 6 for more details.*)

Climb over the wooden and wire fence and continue up the left bank of the stream. The footpath becomes a bit indistinct at times, but if you keep the stream within sight or sound and on your right you can't go far wrong. At the main road cross over and take the side road straight in front of you. Keep to the right as you go through the first yard. Go through the kissing gate in the security fence and then over the bridge into the next yard. Go straight on and make for the gate at the far end.

Climb over the stile by the gate and go along the track until it opens out into the old quarry. Climb up to the higher level on the right as soon as you can and keep going in the same general direction.

(9)   If you look to your right you can get a closer view of the rock face mentioned on the outward journey. This unconformity consists of a lower layer of Carboniferous Limestone, which was formed in the Palaeozoic period under a layer of Jurassic Limestone formed in the Mesozoic period. The Mesozoic period was the age of the giant reptiles when the first birds appeared. If you could get to the interface of the two strata you would probably find remains of shellfish deposited when this was the seabed.

PART OF MURTRY
AQUEDUCT

Follow the bed of the old railway track to the bridge over the stream. Go over this bridge and under the next one. Keep following the track straight on or, if you prefer, you can bear right and follow the bank upstream for a while.

Go under the concrete railway bridge and continue up the valley, past the mill, back to the start.

Continue with Route 3 or 4.

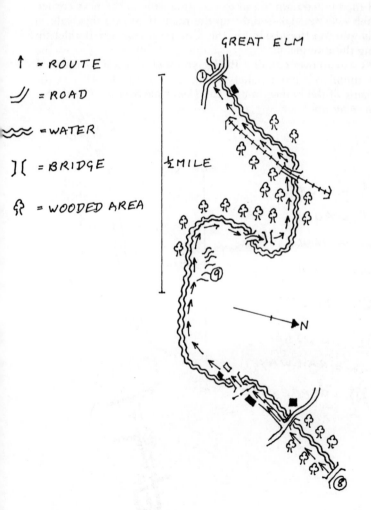

ROUTE 8. Circular Walk from Mells (O.S. 727493) via Buckland Down and Babington House. (6.5 miles.)

(1) Park your car in Mells opposite the Talbot. Walk up New Street, around the church to the north side, through the avenue of yews
(2) and through the ingenious stile. Turn left, go through the gateway by the corner of the Manor garden wall and turn right.

Go up the hill, skirt around the clump of young trees at the top. Follow the hedge around to the left until you reach the stile under the beech tree. Climb over into the corner of the next field
(3) and then go straight ahead to the stone stile in the next corner. Climb over and go straight up the road. If you do this walk in early summer look out for the Common Star Of Bethlehem along these verges.

As you go over Conduit Bridge you will see a long depression
(4) just uphill of, and parallel, to the railway track. This is the remains of the branch line of the *Dorset and Somerset Canal*. (*See Route 6 for details.*)

↑ = ROUTE

⅃ = ROADS

ᴍᴍᴍ = HEDGE

▬ = WALL

🌸 = TREES

)[= BRIDGE

++++ = RAILWAY

§§§§ = DEPRESSION

½ MILE

N

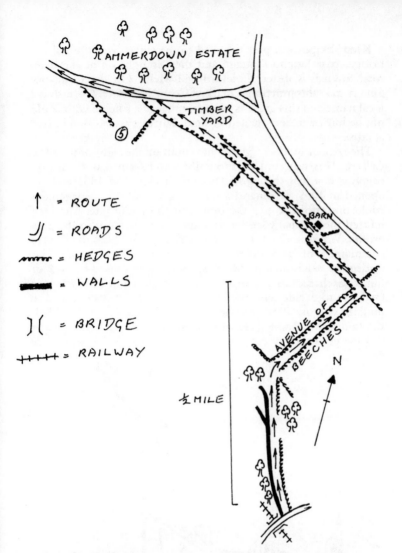

Legend:

↑ = ROUTE

⤴ = ROADS

ᴀᴀᴀᴀ = HEDGES

▬▬▬ = WALLS

](= BRIDGE

++++ = RAILWAY

½ MILE

AMMERDOWN ESTATE

TIMBER YARD

⑤

BARN

AVENUE OF BEECHES

N

Just after the bridge go up the track on the left. At the top, bear right and go through the avenue of beeches. At the end of the avenue, follow the lane as it turns left. At the dog-leg by the barn keep to the lane. Do not go onto the road.

At the end of the lane keep to the left-hand side of the timber yard and then turn left onto the road. The irregularities in the (5) surface of the field on the left are the remains of *Kingsdown Camp*, a medieval settlement. As you go down the hill the long dry-stone wall on the right marks the boundary of the Ammerdown Estate.

Keep straight on, past the road to the right; over the railway bridge; past Jericho Cottage and then straight on at the main road towards Vobster, Coleford and Mells. On the Ordnance Survey map this junction is marked Cornish's Grave. Cornish is a local name and this grave is probably that of a suicide who could not be buried in consecrated ground. Suicides were often buried at crossroads.

(6)   The cement works on the right is built on the sight of the *Mells Colliery*. This was sunk in about 1863 and seemed to be always running at a loss throughout its life. It closed in 1881 and re-opened in 1909. Its financial state was so bad the management could not afford to pay the miners at the going rate. The men refused the company's offer of wages in proportion to the pit's profits. Working conditions were very poor. In 1924 the miners complained of poor ventilation, shortage of pit props and inadequate safety lamps. All these faults were caused by lack of funds. Each month the management stuck a pin into a list of creditors to decide who was to be paid. Receivers were called in on 23rd August 1930 and the colliery was bought by the Mells Estate under Dame F. J. Horner. Despite the workmen agreeing to a ten per cent pay cut, on condition that the deficit was made

NEW STREET

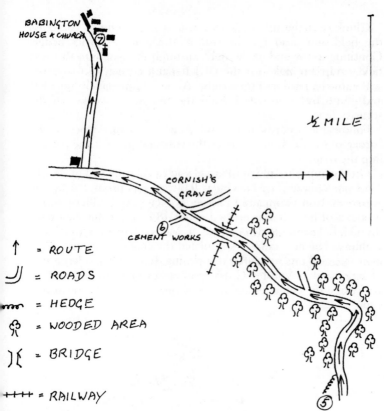

BABINGTON
HOUSE & CHURCH

⑦

½ MILE

CORNISH'S
GRAVE

N

⑥
CEMENT WORKS

↑ = ROUTE

⤴ = ROADS

〰 = HEDGE

🌳 = WOODED AREA

)(= BRIDGE

++++ = RAILWAY

⑤

up when times improved, the Mells Coal Industry Ltd. went into liquidation in 1939. The pit finally closed in 1943.

(7)   When you reach the lodge on the right turn down the drive with the avenue of beeches towards *Babington Church* and *House*.

Babington House was built about 1700 and the church in 1750. A family called Babington lived in the area during the twelfth and fourteenth centuries. There is reference to a chapel in Edward I's time, and later the advowson of the church is said to have belonged to William Lord Botreaux who owned property in Kilmersdon. There are records of him holding a fair in the village which has since disappeared, probably at the time of the Black Death.

At the church you may wish to extend the walk by joining with Route 9. If so follow the directions from point 8 on the map.

If not take the footpath which is on the opposite side of the drive from the church and follow the remnants of a beech avenue and then climb over the stile or through the gate by Charity Cottage into the road.

Climb over the stile opposite. Bear slightly right as you cross the field and head for the tree in the convex corner hedge. Continue to the end of the field, through the gate into the next field, and then make for the far left-hand corner. Get over the stile into the road and turn right. Almost immediately turn left and climb over the stile behind the tree at the corner of the security fence.

Follow the security fence and then the smaller fence to the corner of the field. Climb over the stile and go past the cottage into the road.

(8)   On the opposite side of the road you can see the bed of the old *Newbury Railway*. The Newbury Railway was promoted by the Westbury Iron Company to serve its Newbury Colliery which was east of here. It was opened about 1857 and connected with the GWR Frome–Radstock line at Mells Road near the Mells Colliery. The new railway stimulated the coal owners into sinking three new pits soon after its opening. It also made a large area of limestone at Vobster Cross more accessible. It continued to serve, first the collieries and then the quarries, until its closure in 1966.

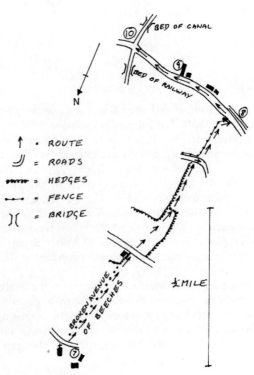

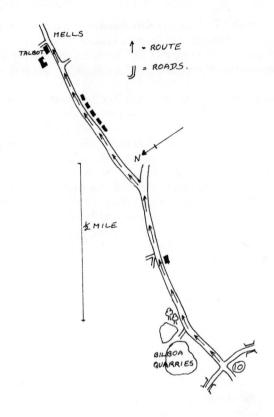

Turn left and follow the road past the houses and converted chapel of Upper Vobster. After passing the more closely packed cottages, if you look back to your right, you can just make out
(9) the top of a bridge which spanned the *Dorset and Somerset Canal*.
(10) When you reach the main road, if you look to your right, you can see another canal bridge. The canal is very clearly defined at this point. If you look to the left what seems to be the brow of the hill is in fact a bridge over the bed of the Newbury Railway.

At the crossroads go straight over, towards Mells. Behind the industrial site on the left is the disused *Bilboa Quarry*, which is also the site of the 240 ft. deep *Bilboa Coal Pit*.

Take the next road to the left, which is signposted to Mells. Keep straight on through the village until you reach the Talbot on the left. (*See Route 1 for details.*)

Continue with Route 8 if you started walking from Kilmersdon, or join Route 1 at point 7.

ROUTE 9. Circular Walk from Kilmersdon (O.S. 696524) **via Cherry Garden Farm and Babington House.** (4 miles.)

(1)   Park your car in the car park 100 yards to the left of and opposite the Jolliffe Arms. Start off by looking around the village.

(2).   The *Old Village Lock Up* was originally built next to the Jolliffe Arms but in 1840 it was moved to its present site on the other side of the road where it is now used as a bus shelter.

On the left, just inside the east gate of the churchyard, there is the Gilson family grave. Were these the descendants of Jack and Jill? This nursery rhyme is reputed to be based on the story of a couple who lived in the village about 350 years ago. They had to climb to the other side of the hill for their water. One day Jack was killed by a falling stone in a nearby quarry. A few days later Jill died in childbirth. The baby boy survived and was raised by the villagers. They called him 'Jill's son'. This gradually changed to Gilson and became his surname.

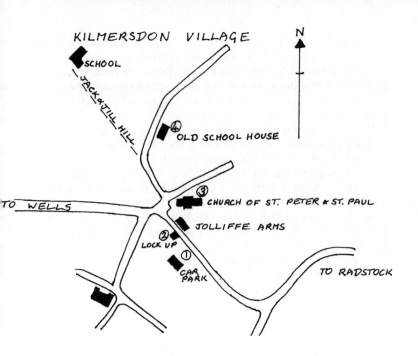

In the right-hand corner of the churchyard there is another gravestone which I find interesting because of the amount of personal details it records. It reads: 'Sacred to the memory of Anne Abraham who expired on the 27th March 1849 in the 104th year of her age. Her physical powers were preserved to her nearly unimpared to the two last years of her existance. Previously to which she regularly walked a distance of a mile and a half to perform such light work as with a due regard to her advanced age she was at her own express desire, still suffered at intervals to engage in. For a laudable feeling of independence she always resolutely refused parochial relief.'

3) The *Church of St. Peter & St. Paul* with its ornate twelfth century tower has an abundance of gargoyles and other carved figures around its walls. Some are fierce, some are amusing. Some laugh, some frown. There is an angel holding her skirt, a man riding a horse and two laughing masks. The *Lych Gate* is triangular and has a stone roof.

4) As you come out through the lych gate bear left as you cross the road and walk up Alms Lane. The *Old School House*, which was built in the early eighteenth century, is up here on the right. It faces the hill which Jack and Jill are reputed to have climbed.

On the horizon to the east of the village is *Ammerdown Tower* which was built in 1885 for Lord Hylton as a memorial to Thomas Jolliffe. His neighbour, John Turner, was so jealous he built one thirty feet higher. It did not last and the only trace of it left today is the name 'Turner's Tower' on the telephone and post box.

Retrace your steps to the village centre.

After exploring the village go up the side street opposite the phone box by the road from the church. When the road turns sharp right go up the No Through Road which is in front of you but slightly to your left. As you do so the house on the right is

(5)   *The Manor House*.

(6)   At the corner of Walton Farmyard climb over the stile into the field on your left. Turn right, and skirt around the silage pit to the stile in the corner of the field. When I walked this route they had peacocks running around the yard.

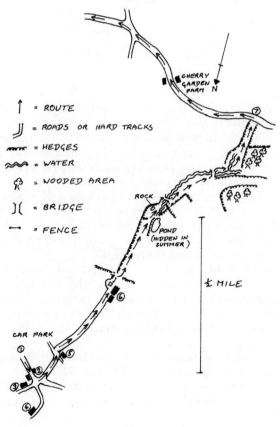

↑	= ROUTE
∫∫	= ROADS OR HARD TRACKS
⌐⌐⌐	= HEDGES
∿∿	= WATER
♣	= WOODED AREA
)(	= BRIDGE
⟼	= FENCE

CHERRY GARDEN FARM

N

ROCK

POND (HIDDEN IN SUMMER)

¼ MILE

CAR PARK

48

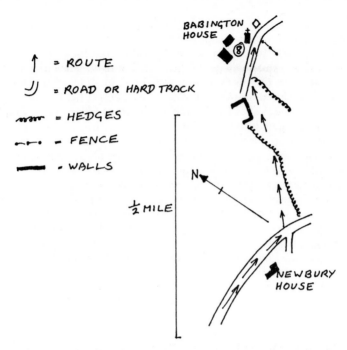

Climb over the stile, go past the gate, turn left and continue on up through the valley, walking on the right-hand side of the hedge. Follow the hedge through the narrow part of the field, through the broken hedge and past the rock in the bank on the left. Climb over the stile in the corner of the field and walk straight ahead. Cross over to the right-hand side of the stream by the soil bridge. Keep following the stream and then cross over to the left by the bridge which is level with the wood on the right.

Go upstream for a short distance until you cross over a small stream which flows down from your left (it probably runs dry in the summer). Climb up the field to the left hand corner of the wood in front of you.

(7)   Go up the old lane and climb over the stile into the road.

Turn left and follow the road past Cherry Garden Farm. Keep straight on at the first road junction and then bear left at the fork.

After passing Newbury House, climb over the stiles and the footbridge which are on the left, opposite the road to Newbury. Head across the field, at about 45 degrees, towards Babington House. Climb over the stile by the kink in the hedge into the next field. Keep heading for the house as you cross the field and go through the gate in the corner into the lane. Turn right until you

(8)   reach the church.

At this point you may wish to extend the walk by joining with Route 8. If so follow the directions from point 7.

If not, take the path between the church and the cemetery. Go through the small gate and follow the left hand fence down into the valley. In the bottom corner of the field climb over the two stiles at each end of the footbridge into the next field.

Walk straight ahead and make for the stone pillars. Go through the broken gate into the wood.

This mixed woodland contains mature specimens of beech, oak, ash, lime, sweet chestnut, horse chestnut, sycamore, holly, yew, box and field maple with a shrub layer of laurel, hazel and elder. There are also signs of deer, so keep your eyes open.

Go down through the wood until two streams on the left meet. Go over the footbridge. As you do so look up the second stream at the tree which has roots in both banks. Turn right in the field and follow the edge of the wood until you reach the double pylon in the hedge. Cross the field and make for the church.

Climb over the stile into the next field and follow the right hand hedge to the stile into the road. Cross over the road and turn left. Follow the road around to the right into the village.

BABINGTON HOUSE AND CHURCH

KILMERSDON

↑ = ROUTE

⌐J = ROAD OR HARD TRACK

∽ = HEDGES

•—• = FENCES

∼∼ = WATER

🌳 = WOODED AREA

N

½ MILE

BABINGTON HOUSE

CEMETRY

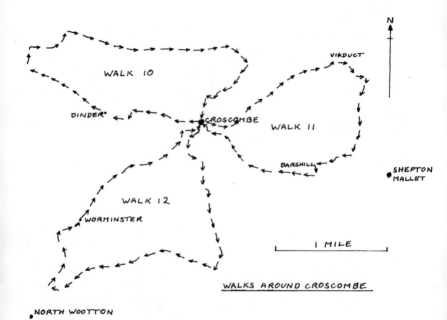

WALKS AROUND CROSCOMBE

Croscombe lies on the southern edge of the Mendip Hills, about half way between Wells and Shepton Mallet. It owed its earlier prosperity to the woollen industry. As that trade declined other ventures were tried such as silk, mining for minerals and chemical manufacturing. Today most of the residents either work on the land or commute to neighbouring towns.

Croscombe may not seem very attractive to motorists driving along its narrow, busy main road, but if you take to side roads and leave your car you can admire the picturesque and historic buildings set in the beautiful surrounding countryside.

Dinder, which lies to the west of Croscombe, is another picturesque but smaller village, with a roadside stream and stone built cottages.

COUNTRYSIDE NEAR NORTH WOOTTON

The high Mendips to the north, are made up of small fielded farmland and wooded combes, while the countryside to the south is mainly farmland with vineyards on the warmer south-facing slopes at Pilton and North Wooton.

The old woollen town of Shepton Mallet was once the centre of a thriving cloth-manufacturing industry but now the biggest employer is Showerings, the cider and perry makers. There are also several small industrial estates being constructed around the town. Recently excavations uncovered a Roman burial ground.

The small city of Wells marks the western boundary of the area described. It contains a lovely Cathedral, an ancient Bishop's Palace and Deanery, with wonderful old houses built for the clergy, very largely unspoilt except by the inexhaustible traffic.

ROUTE 10. Circular walk from Croscombe (O.S. 590445) **via Dinder and Kings Castle Wood.** (5 miles.)

(1).   Park your car in Fayre Way at the top of Church Street. Walk down Fayre Way to the last bungalow on the right. Climb over the stone stile by the public seat and cross the field to the stile in the opposite hedge. Climb diagonally in the next field to where two sets of power lines cross. Look at the length of the lines which span the valley. The fields on the opposite side of the

(2)   valley show very clearly the effects of the old strip lynchets cultivation system on the landscape.

Climb over the stile in the corner of the field and follow the left-hand hedge of the next field. Go through the gate and turn left in the road. At the T-junction turn right into the village of Dinder. This is another very attractive village with its Dulcote Stone cottages and roadside stream.

When the main street turns left, you turn right and then follow this road around to the left past Derrick Close to the church.

(3)   The *Church of St. Michael and All Angels* was formerly a Norman Chapel. In 1460 it was extended in the perpendicular style and the chancel rebuilt in 1872. On the south side of the church is a very old distorted yew tree.

DINDER

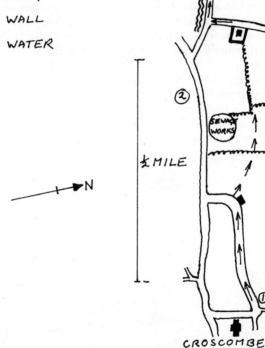

↑ = ROUTE

⌡ = ROADS

〰 = HEDGES

▬ = WALL

〰 = WATER

DINDER

½ MILE

→N

②

SEWAGE WORKS

③

①

CROSCOMBE

If you don't visit the church, go straight on. At the end of the road climb over the stile in the far right-hand corner of the yard. Cross the field, past a telegraph pole and make for the kissing gate which is to the right of the oak.

If you look to your right you can see Second World War pill boxes on the hillside above you.

Head for the far right-hand corner of the next field. Climb over the stile or go through the gate into the next field and follow the hedge. Go past the five barred gate and then go through the kissing gate where the hedge bends slightly to the left.

Go over the footbridge, turn left, follow the footpath across the corner of the field and then follow the hedge to the far left-hand corner of the field.

(4)   Go through the kissing gate and bear right across the next field, past the single oak, to the gates in the opposite hedge. Go through the kissing gate into the lane and turn right. Follow the lane through a small wood to the top of the hill.

Climb over the metal stile and follow the left-hand hedge. In the corner of the field go through the gate and then about turn so that you are following the lane with a fence on your right and a hedge on your left. When I walked this route last the golf course was being extended into the field on the right so the fence may have been removed when you walk this route.

FOOTPATH FROM DINDER

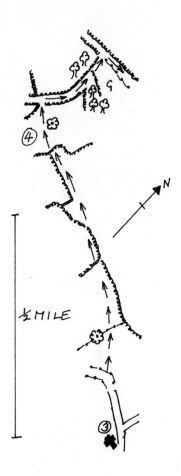

↑ = ROUTE

⌡ = ROAD

〰 = HEDGE

•—•— = FENCE

🌳 = WOODED AREA

〰 = LANE
〰

🌸 = TREE

G = GOLF COURSE
EXTENSION

½ MILE

N

④

③

57

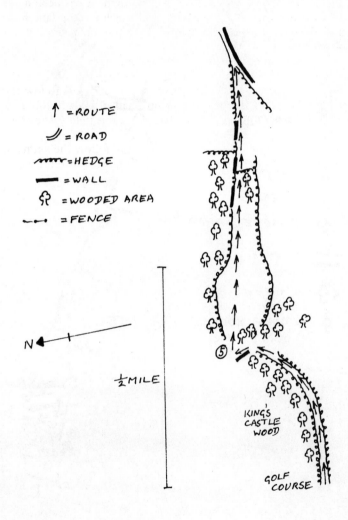

↑ = ROUTE

// = ROAD

∿∿∿ = HEDGE

▬ = WALL

♣ = WOODED AREA

•–•– = FENCE

N

½ MILE

⑤

KING'S CASTLE WOOD

GOLF COURSE

The track you are on was once an ancient coach road which was used extensively in the eighteenth century by travellers wishing to avoid paying tolls on the main roads. On the right Kings Castle Wood with its Iron Age Settlement has been made into a nature reserve. If you wish you can leave the lane here, follow the paths through the reserve and rejoin the route at point 5 on the map.

(5) If not follow the lane until it climbs through a wood. In the wood go through the gate and follow the dry stone wall on the left to the top. At the top turn right and more or less follow the left-hand hedge of the 'leg of mutton' shaped field. If you look over your right shoulder as you walk along this field you can see Glastonbury Tor in the middle distance.

Go through the gate into the next field and follow the left hand wall and hedge. Go through the gate in the corner into the road.

Go past the wall and shed and then go through the gate into the field on the right. There is another Second World War pill box in front of you, but slightly to your left.

Turn left and make for the far right-hand corner of the field. Go through the gate and take the path down into the hollow. As you climb down into the hollow, if you look back to your right, you will see the remains of an old lime kiln. (For a description of how lime was made see Route 7.)

(6)

There are several large lumps of concrete tipped into the disused quarry by the kiln. These are the remains of anti-tank barriers which were erected between the pill boxes as a defence against German invasion in the 1939-45 war.

Keep straight on through the hollow to the corner of the field. Go through the gate into the road and turn left. Follow the road straight on. Just past the tree in the right-hand hedge climb over the stone stile on the right.

Bear slightly left as you cross the field and get over the stone stile into the next field. Keep bearing left in the next field but pass to the right of the electric pole. Make for the far left-hand corner and go through the gate into the lane.

Turn right and follow the lane until it starts down into the valley. Soon after it starts to drop, turn into the grassy lane on the right. Climb over the stone stile on the left and go down the hill over two stiles and you are back to the start.

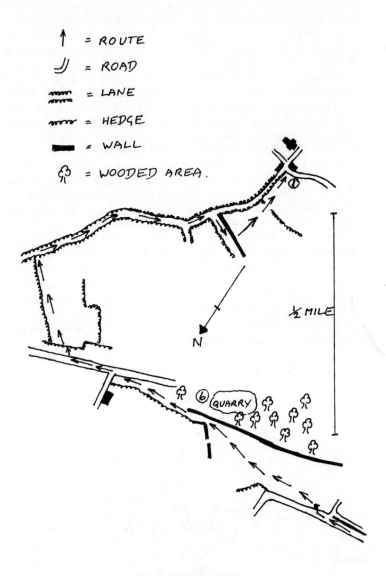

= ROUTE
= ROAD
= LANE
= HEDGE
= WALL
= WOODED AREA.

½ MILE

N

6 QUARRY

61

ROUTE 11. Circular walk from Croscombe via Ham Woods and the Darshill district of Shepton Mallet. (5 miles.)

(1)   Park your car near the junction at the top of Church Street and Fayre Way. Walk across the top of Church Street and as you do so notice how the walls of the house on the corner of Fayre Way are rounded to fit the line of the road. There are also interesting masks over each window.

Go along Poundfold, turn left at the top of Rock Street, and then right off Thrupe Lane to go along Boards Lane. When the road turns sharp right go straight ahead and climb over the wall with built-in steps. Follow the wall and then the fence on the right. At the corner of the fence go straight on. As you go down the slope into the valley the main road is on your right.

At the bottom of the slope, turn left. Climb over the stile by the gate and then carry on up the wooded valley. You are now in *Ham Woods*. After you pass through a dark coniferous area the woods become more open. When the track you are following turns sharp right, go straight on but keep to the left-hand bank of the stream. (When I last walked this route I had to make a small detour to the left to skirt around fallen trees.)

Years ago Nancy Camel, an unfortunate recluse who was supposed to be a witch, lived in these woods. She made her living by knitting stockings, even on Sundays. She was regarded as an object of ridicule and fear. Badly behaved children were told that Nancy would take them away if they did not mend their ways. One night she disappeared during a thunder storm. That night locals said they heard the sounds of galloping horses, creaking wheels, cracking whips, piercing screams and devilish laughter. In the morning, when they could not find her, they concluded that the Devil had claimed his own.

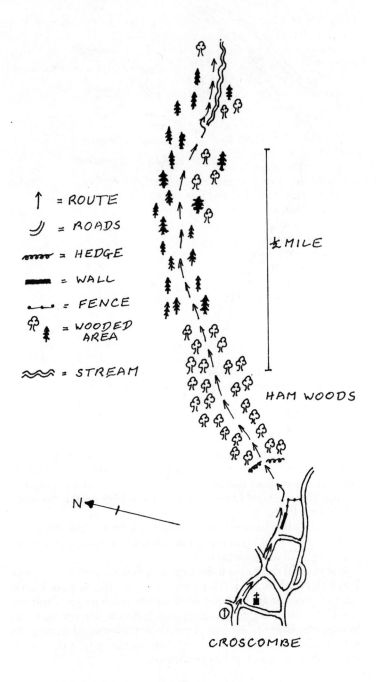

= ROUTE

= ROADS

= HEDGE

= WALL

= FENCE

= WOODED AREA

= STREAM

½ MILE

HAM WOODS

N

CROSCOMBE

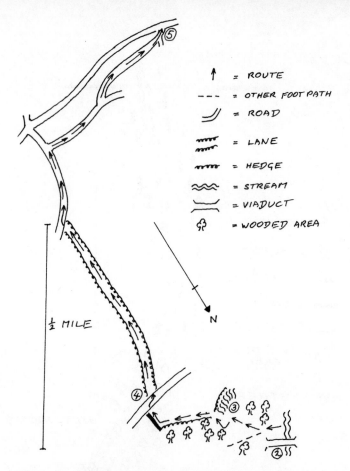

(2)   When the *Viaduct* comes into view just after the footpath sign follow the path over the stream and walk straight ahead. In summer the viaduct is almost hidden by foliage. It used to carry the old Somerset and Dorset Railway from 1874 until it closed on 6th March 1966.

Iron and other minerals were mined near here in the nineteenth century. About 70 yards further on I found a strange metal frame. Is it part of an old mineral truck?

Just beyond this point follow the less defined path to the right. I had to crawl under a fallen tree to do so. If you pass a small tumble-down stone building on your left you have gone too far.

(3)   Follow this path into an old quarry. It is quite interesting to see how nature is gradually reclaiming her territory and healing the man-made scars. When I walked here in the spring the rubble strewn floor was a carpet of primroses.

Turn left just before the rock face and then keep turning right. Climb the steps cut into the hillside. At the top climb over the stile and turn left. Follow the left-hand hedge and then wall to the far corner of the field. Climb over the stile into the road and (4) turn right. Turn left down Rubble Lane.

Turn right at the end of the lane and follow the road down into the Bowlish district of Shepton Mallet. Just before you reach the main road turn right up Ham Lane. Turn left by the Old Manor with its mounting block by the wall, and go down the hill to the (5) main road.

There were four major factories straddling the river in this highly industrialised community during the eighteenth and nineteenth centuries. They first produced woollen material and then, when the woollen trade declined, converted to silk and crepe production. This change in production could not save the factories as trade continued to decline. This decline caused great hardship and led to unrest and civil disobedience as skilled craftsmen were forced to work in road gangs or become beggars. Whole families starved and riots broke out in 1843. At this time Lower Darshill Mill was burnt down. The site was eventually cleared to make way for sewage works in the 1890s.

Middle Darshill was the last one to cease trading in 1913. The buildings were demolished in the late 1970s

At the main road turn left and then cross over to the footpath sign on the other side. Climb over the stile and up the hill. At the top climb over the stile and turn right.

At the end of the houses get over the stile and go straight across the field. Follow the right hand hedges of the next two fields, and then go straight across the third.

Climb over the metal stile into the field where the Clay Pigeon Club meets. Follow the left-hand hedge to the corner, go straight on and then make for the lone tree. The arches you can see in the opposite hillside are part of the sewage works built on the site of the *Lower Darshill Mill*.

Go past the tree to the stile under the tree in the far hedge. Climb over the stile and bear right across the next field, keeping more or less to the same contour line. Climb over the stile in the top left corner of the narrow part of the field. Turn right and follow the fence and then the hedge and stream to the garden wall.

(6)   The two bungalows in front of you are built on the site of J.E. Woods & Co. *Chemical Works*. In 1865 Sir Charles Bright started mining for various minerals in the surrounding hills. The main mineral sought was iron ore. The chemical works were established to manufacture chemicals reclaimed during the processing of the ore, e.g. white lead. Local tradesmen welcomed this promising new venture during the decline of the woollen industry. They offered credit for goods required to establish the business. It cost £27,000 to start trading but the venture soon failed leaving massive debts.

Climb over the stile and skirt the wall to the road. Go over the bridge to the main road.

This rather attractive bridge was erected as access to the chemical works and was named Prosperity Bridge. When the chemical venture failed it was nick-named Folly Bridge. Hence 'Folly Bridge Cottages'.

(7)   The *early Tudor House* facing you on the right was the Rectorial Manor and may have been donated to the local clergy by Abbot John Selwood of Glastonbury. To the left, there is a plaque on the wall where a stand pipe was installed by The Croscombe Water Company. The plaque reads '*Drink and Thank*'.

(8)   Cross over the road and turn left. The *Old Mill* on the left is on the site of the earliest mill fed by Croscombe stream as it flowed through the village. The river was originally called Doulting Water but was changed to Croscombe Stream when the village

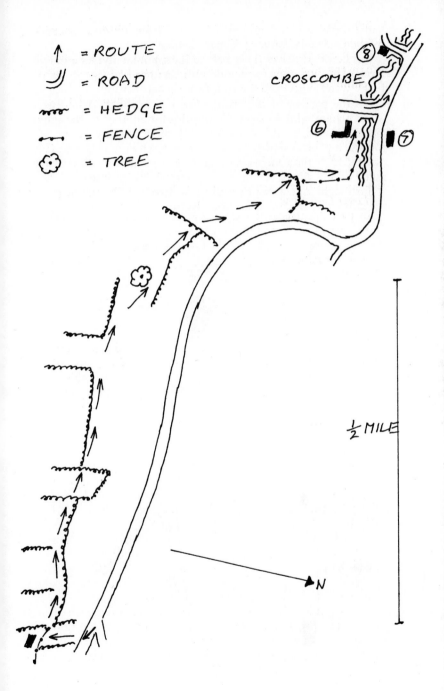

had a thriving woollen industry. It was renamed River Sheppey by the Ordnance Survey officials in about 1884.

Just before the river flows behind the school it divides into two levels. This was done to provide sufficient head of water to drive, first a water wheel and then a turbine in another mill.

(9)   On the parapet of the bridge downstream of the school is a stone plaque which marks the position of another of the stand pipes installed by the Croscombe Water Company. There are four such plaques which have been restored by the villagers. This one reads 'If thou knewest the gift of God thou wouldest have asked of him and he would have given thee living water'.

Turn right and start to climb Rock Street. (I like the name of the cottage at the junction: Rock Bottom.) Go through the gate on the left, through the churchyard to the church.

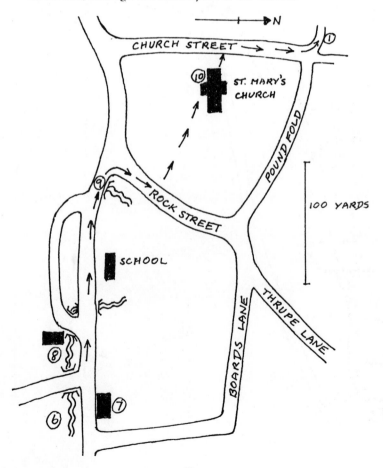

(10)   *St. Mary's Church* is an architectural gem. It is mainly fifteenth and sixteenth century and built of Dolomitic Conglomerate and Doulting Stone. It has a spire instead of the more common Somerset tower. This spire was rebuilt when the original one was hit by lightning in 1936. The quarry from which the original stone was obtained was reopened so that the new would blend in with the old.

The oldest surviving part of the church is the outer doorway of the south porch. At the north-east end is the clergy vestry which was built as a chapel by John Carter of Exeter sometime between 1507 and 1512. It has a ribbed tunnel-vault. At the south-west end is the treasury. It is two-storeyed. The ground floor has small barred windows and the upper floor larger windows. It was here that the seven Guilds of Croscombe met. The Guilds were: The Young Men, The Maidens, The Webbers (weavers), The Fullers, The Hogglers (labourers), The Archers and The Wives. In the sixteenth and seventeenth centuries it was used as the parish armoury and at one time the parish lock up.

There are hardly any pieces of wood inside which are not covered in mainly Jacobean carvings. The rood screen has two tiers of two-light openings. The most prominent feature is the Royal Coat of Arms. There are many obelisks both over and under the upper arches. The pulpit, dated 1616, is large with a tester to match. They are both richly carved and gilded. The box pews are also beautifully carved. Croscombe's weaving heritage is depicted in some of the figures carved in the roof. There are some shown unfurling bolts of cloth.

As you leave the church turn right and, when you reach Church Street, right again to arrive back at Fayre Way.

PEW GATE IN CROSCOMBE CHURCH

ROUTE 12. Circular walk from Croscombe via North Wootton (5.5 miles.)

(1)   Park your car at the top of Church Street and Fayre Way. Walk down Church Street. On the right hand side, opposite the

(2)   church, is the old *Tythe Barn*. It's the smallest one I have ever seen.

Most of the villagers were employed in cottage industries. As time went on the trade carried out in each house changed. For example, one of the cottages near the tythe barn was an undertaker's and before that cheese was made there.

(3)   *The Bull Terrier*, formerly called the Rose & Crown, was built in the latter half of the fifteenth century. It was granted its first licence to sell ale in 1612 and it can therefore claim to be one of the oldest Somerset pubs. Although it was modified in the eighteenth century, it still retains many of its mediaeval features and is an excellent place to stop for lunch.

Before the present main road was laid the route through the village was very narrow and winding. When authorities tried to move the ancient *Croscombe Cross* to make more room for the first traction engines, the villagers picketed it to prevent them doing so. Mabs Holland summed up the incident very well in her poem:

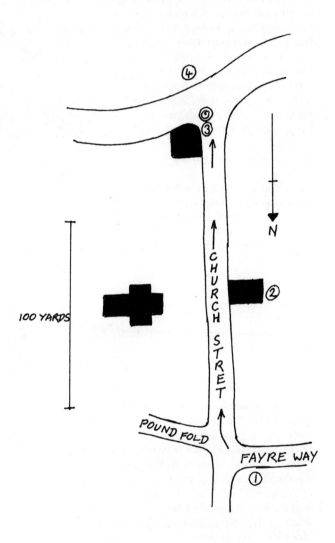

100 YARDS

④

⑤
③

N

CHURCH STRET

②

POUND FOLD

FAYRE WAY

①

CROSCOMBE CROSS

In days gone by, Way Wardens sought
To move our ancient Cross
Each turning up at daybreak
Wi' a dray and shire hoss
To car' away our Moniment
Our Calv'ry, stone by stone
'Til village blacksmith hollered
'Hey! Thee leave thik Cross alone!
He've a-stood fer cench'ries, aye,
Long 'for our Church Were built.
Pack up thy gear and toddle off
Or thee might jist get kill'd!'

Said t'others, 'We got orders, see
Thik Cross be in the way . . .'
Set just one hand' growled blacksmith
'And I vow thee'lt rue the day!'
Soon other folk had gathered there
To see what was the fuss—
Twudden very ofter, see,
They'd heard the blacksmith cuss.
'Remove our Cross? Not likely!'
Parson's wife cried wi' a stamp
Of her button-booted-size-ten-feet
As she let fly wi' her gamp.

'Shame on you!' 'Vandals!' 'Villains!'
How the angry roar
Echoed 'round the hills of Croscombe
As along the streets did pour
Notaries, lackeys, labourers
Their children and their wives—
(Some wi' more sense than Wardens
Would ha' run to save their lives!)
There were Chandlers and bakers
And a girl who needled lace
While at the rear an undertaker strode—
More leisurely of pace.

'Back off . . .' they urged the Wardens.
'Try and make us . . .' answered they
Then, as if by common signal,
Each side leapt into the fray
Battling through the morning
Far into the afternoon
Until the daylight faded
And they found there was no moon.
Then thirty stalwart Croscombe lads
Settled down into redoubt
While the girl who needled lace stood by
To give a warning shout.

E'er morning came a banner bright
Wi' lettering o' gold
Flew o'er the Cross – 'BE FAITHFUL'—
Was the legend there it told.
Twice down was torn the banner,
Shaft of cross and filial, too.
But the villagers of Croscombe
To their principles were true.
Way Wardens soon were vanquished
And they quit with this advice—
'Before you make old Croscombe cross
Think twice, my friends, think twice.'

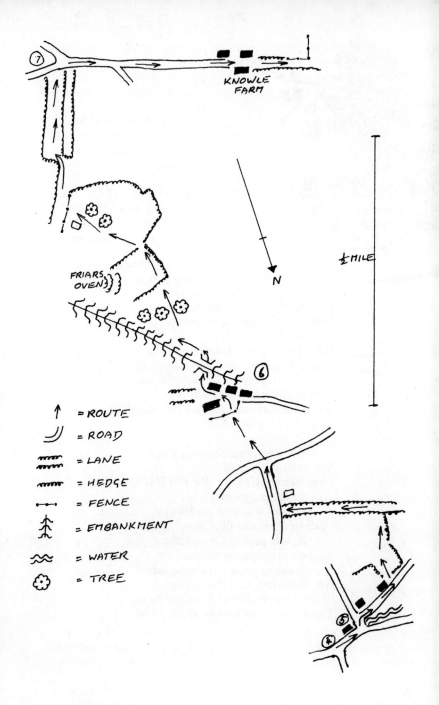

KNOWLE
FARM

FRIARS
OVEN

N

½ MILE

↑ = ROUTE

⌒ = ROAD

〜 = LANE

〜 = HEDGE

•—•—• = FENCE

⚘ = EMBANKMENT

〜〜 = WATER

❀ = TREE

74

(4)   The building and the chimney on the opposite side of the main road was part of a *Mill* which originally stretched half way across the road: No wonder they had traffic problems! It was first powered by water wheel and then by steam. Apparently the old boiler is still in the surviving building.

The plaque by the roadside here was recently restored by the villagers. It was originally installed, with a stand pipe, by the Croscombe Water Company. It reads 'Whosoever shall drink this water shall thirst again. But whosoever shall drink of the water that I shall give him shall never thirst'.

Turn right along the main road. Past the post office, which used to be a hat factory. Cross over the road and turn left over the
(5)   bridge by *The Old Forge*. Turn right in front of the Advent Church. Go up the hill and turn left by the white cottage on the left. Cross the tarmac and climb over the stile into the field.

Make for the top right hand corner of the field and go through the gate into the lane. Turn left, follow the lane, and then turn right on the road by the reservoir.

At the top of the hill go through the gate to your right on the opposite side of the road. Bear slightly left as you go down the hill and go through the gate into the farmyard. In the mid
(6)   nineteenth century this farm, *Dungeon Farm*, was used by smugglers. Silk and brandy were brought in from Bristol and the Severn Estuary. The silk was knotted and hidden in sacks of potatoes and the brandy hidden among the cheeses. The locals who informed the excise men of these activities were said to have been rewarded with cattle from the farm.

Turn left just past the long building and follow the track of the old lane. Go into the field on the right and then cut across to the right-hand side of the field. Go through the tunnel under the old railway embankment.

Turn left, follow the embankment for a while and then cut across the field to go between the second and third trees. Climb over the stone stile in the short hedge in front of you.

Go straight up the field, past the rock formation called *Friars Oven*, to the right hand corner. Go through the gap in the hedge and bear left. Go through the trees in the middle of the field and pass to the right of the drinking trough.

In the corner of the field climb over the newly erected fence. (When I last walked this route there was a lot of building activity going on to your left, so the arrangement of fences and gates etc. may change at this point.) Turn right through the gate and start down the hill. Go through the gap into the next field and follow
(7)   the right-hand hedge to the gate into the road.

Turn right and follow the 'No Through Road' to Knowle Farm. Go through the farm into the lane beyond. Follow the lane and then the hardcore track until you reach the wire fence. Go through the gate and turn left across the field to the footbridge by the telegraph pole.

Go over the bridge and stiles into the next field and turn right. Follow the ridge in the field, past the drinking trough, and then make for the bottom corner of the field. Go through the gate into the next field.

Climb over the gate on the right into the next field, turn left and follow the hedge and fence up the hill and past the garden until you reach a gate and stile into a lane. Climb over the stile into the lane and turn right. Follow the lane through the valley until you reach the road. The milk stand by the roadside is a reminder of when milk was collected in churns before the more hygienic tankers.

Go straight across the road and follow the lane by the stream until it turns sharp left. Climb over the barbed-wire fence into the field on the right. Go straight across the field, over the stile, and across the next field. Walk across two more fields with the fence, ditch and trees on your right.

(8) Go through the gate in the corner and then straight down the lane to the main road. Turn right, over the bridge, and then take the road to the left.

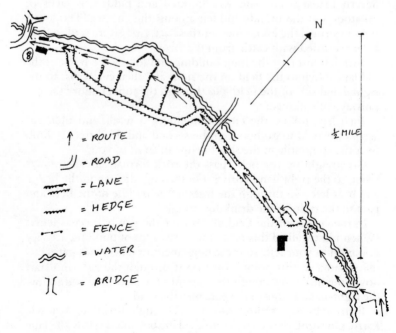

N

½ MILE

↑ = ROUTE
⌐J = ROAD
~~~~ = LANE
~~~ = HEDGE
•–•–• = FENCE
~~~ = WATER
)(= BRIDGE

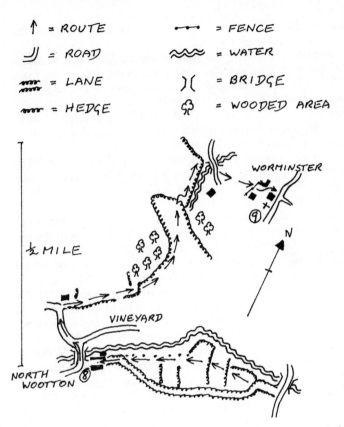

Legend:
↑ = ROUTE
⌐ = ROAD
~ = LANE
~ = HEDGE
•—• = FENCE
~~~ = WATER
)(= BRIDGE
♧ = WOODED AREA

WORMINSTER

½ MILE

N

VINEYARD

NORTH
WOOTTON

When the road turns left by a petrol pump, turn right, go through a black gate and up two steps into the garden. When I walked this route for the first time I checked with the owner of the house to make sure this is the footpath. It is. Go down the path to the far end of the garden.

Climb over the stile into the vineyard and follow the right-hand hedge into the next one. Go through the small gate into the field on the left. Turn right and follow the fence. Climb over the stile into the wood. After a short distance, leave the wood via the stile into a field. Follow the edge of the wood around to the right until you can see the next field. Cut across the field you are in, to the far right-hand corner.

Go through the gate into the next field and follow the right-hand hedge and stream. One year the farmer was unwillingly feeding the local wild deer population with maize from this field.

Enter the next field and turn right onto a concrete drive. Go over the bridge and climb over the fence into the field on the left.

Climb up the field to the gate into the farmyard. Follow the yellow arrows through the yard.

(9)   Behind the farmhouse is an *Ancient Wayside Cross*. If you make a slight detour as you leave the yard you can see it from the road. In 1877 only two steps and the socket existed. The shaft was added at a later date, but prior to 1935.

There is a much disputed legend that Bishop Jocelyn of Wells killed a dragon or serpent which was terrorising this hamlet of Worminster. Was this the 'Worm' of *Worminster*?

Worminster has been one of the prebendal estates of Wells Cathedral since Bishop Giso was made the prebendary. He was the last of the thirteen Bishops of Wells and was in office from 1061 to 1080.

Turn left at the road and, at the first bend, go up some steps and over a stile into the field on the right. Climb across to the top left-hand corner and get over the awkward stile into a farm track. Turn left and, when the track turns right, carry straight on through the gate into the field. Follow the left-hand hedge. On the left, in the middle distance, you can see the outskirts of Wells.

Go through the gateway into the next field, bear slightly right and make for the house on the horizon as you go down the slope.

(10) Cross over the bed of the old railway track via two stiles

This was part of the *East Somerset Railway*. The East Somerset Railway first opened with a broad gauge line from Witham to Shepton Mallet in 1858. Brunel allowed enough land for a double track when he surveyed for this stretch of line. Only a single track was laid. The line was extended to Wells in 1862. At one stage they planned to route the railway through Croscombe but they had to build it further south because of opposition from landowners. It was taken over by the Great Western Railway in 1874. It closed in 1964.

Keep to the right of the clump of trees as you climb the slope. Climb over the stile and follow the path to the road. Turn right,

(11) past Churchill House, to the cross-roads. Go straight over the cross-roads, and down the hill. Turn left by the first bungalow on the left. Follow the path down to the main road. Cross over and turn right.

Follow the main road back into the centre of the village. Opposite The George, by the bridge you crossed near the start of this walk, is another plaque recently restored. It reads, 'There is a river, the stream whereof shall make glad the City of God'.

When you reach The Bull Terrier turn back up Church Street to the start.

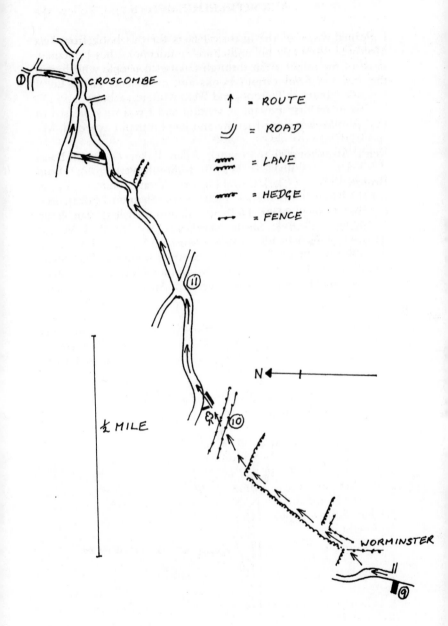

CROSCOMBE

↑ = ROUTE

◡ = ROAD

〰 = LANE

⌒ = HEDGE

•—• = FENCE

N ←——|——————

½ MILE

WORMINSTER

⑪

⑩

⑨

①

ACKNOWLEDGEMENTS

I gleaned many of the historical facts for this book from *Old Mendip* by Robin Atthill and church guidebooks; but I obtained most of the information through talking to people who live in the area and from various books and documents in the Local History Library at Taunton, and Wells Museum Library.

This is my first attempt at writing and I was very pleased to find people even more friendly and helpful than I expected. My special thanks to:

Keith Armstrong (Croscombe); Allan Baker & Kevin Bates (Melksham); Graham & Peg Best (South Petherton); David Bromwich & Liz Clark (Local History Library, Taunton); Ray & Rikki Clarke (Croscombe); Fred Davis (Shepton Mallet); Rod Griffin (Calne); Mabs Holland (Shepton Mallet); Ian Jones (Hilmarton); Rod & Sheila Matthews (Yeovil); Paul Merritt (Devizes); Graeme Osborn (Wells Museum Library); Liz Russell (Lockeridge); Mavis Secrett (Croscombe); Audrey & Stan Shore (Henley); Chris & Pete Stagg (Midsomer Norton); Sue Stagg (Calne); Bob Thornton (West Overton); Anita Yearsly (Kendal).

STAR OF BETHLEHEM